Laughing Giraffe

Other books by Mwenye Hadithi and Adrienne Kennaway:

978 0 340 56565 0 (PB)

978 0 340 41391 3 (PB)

978 0 340 40912 1 (PB)

978 0 340 62685 6 (PB)

978 0 340 51624 9 (PB)

978 0 340 48698 6 (PB)

978 0 340 58048 6 (PB)

978 0 340 94521 6 (HB)

First published in 2008 by Hodder Children's Books

Text copyright © Bruce Hobson 2008
Illustrations copyright © Adrienne Kennaway 2008

Hodder Children's Books, 338 Euston Road, London, NW1 3BH

Hodder Children's Books Australia
Level 17/207 Kent Street, Sydney, NSW 2000

The right of Bruce Hobson to be identified as the author and
Adrienne Kennaway as the illustrator of this Work has been asserted
by them in accordance with the Copyright, Designs and Patents Act 1988.

A catalogue record of this book is available from the British Library.

ISBN: 978 0 340 94519 3

Printed in China

Hodder Children's Books is a division of Hachette Children's Books.
An Hachette Livre UK Company.

Laughing Giraffe

Written by
Mwenye Hadithi

Illustrated by
Adrienne Kennaway

Hodder
Children's
Books

a division of Hachette Children's Books

In the days long ago when Warthog was beautiful and Hippo lived only on the land, Giraffe was the noisiest animal on the Great African Plain.

He SHOUTED a lot and he laughed all the time.

In the Lucky Bean Tree, where the little weaver birds rested, Giraffe would **POP!** his head up through the branches and take a mouthful of leaves and

HAW! HAW! HAW! with laughter.

The little weaver birds fell out of the tree with fright.

In the Wild Date Palms,
where the little sunbirds snoozed,
Giraffe would

POP!
his head up through the leaves
and take a mouthful of ripe fruit and

HAW! HAW!
HAW! with laughter.

The little
sunbirds
were thrown
out of their
nests.

In the Tall Reeds, where the little kingfishers perched, Giraffe would

POP!

his head up through the branches and take a mouthful of water and

HAW! HAW! HAW! with laughter.

The little kingfishers tumbled into the water.

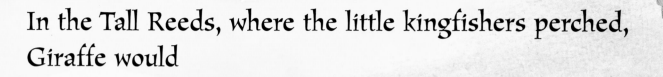

One day, when the little egrets were
sitting on a Toothbrush Bush, enjoying
the warm sun, Giraffe gave them such
a fright that the Littlest Egret
fell into a mud puddle.

"HAW!

HAW!

HAW!" laughed Giraffe.

"Giraffe!" the Littlest Egret scolded. "You are loud and noisy and mean. Anybody can be noisy all the time. Even I could be as noisy as you if I wanted to."

"You? That's a laugh," shouted Giraffe.

"Then we will have a competition to see who has the loudest voice," the Littlest Egret challenged him.

"Agreed,"
laughed Giraffe.

"Then let us go
into the forest
and we will shout back
to the plain and see
who has the loudest voice,"
said the Littlest Egret.

"And I shall judge the competition," offered Kudu.

The sun was just above Giraffe's left knee
when they passed the Lucky Bean Tree
where the weavers rested.

The sun
was just above
Giraffe's neck
when they passed
under the Wild Date
Palms where the
sunbirds snoozed.

And it was just behind Giraffe's head
when they finally stopped by the Tall Reeds
where the little kingfishers were fishing.

"Now you must shout and tell the animals on the plain what you want for dinner," said Kudu.

"Easy!" yelled Giraffe. "I want leafy thorn-tree tips for my dinner!"

And in a voice that could just be heard above
the breeze the Littlest Egret shouted,
"I want little brown beetles for my dinner!"

As they turned to head home,
the little kingfishers flew high in the
air singing, "Little brown beetles!"

As they passed the
Wild Date Palms,
the little sunbirds
flitted from flower
to flower singing,
"Little brown
beetles!"

And as they passed
the Lucky Bean Tree, the
little weavers were chattering,
"Little brown beetles!"

When they finally reached the plain, Kudu asked the giraffes, "What have you got for Giraffe's dinner tonight?"

"Today we have crunchy Toothbrush Bush tips," said the giraffes.

"But I wanted leafy Thorn-tree tips!" shouted Giraffe, crossly.

"Well, why didn't you say something?" said the giraffes.

Kudu then asked the egrets, "What have you got
for the Littlest Egret's dinner tonight?"

"Little brown beetles," said the egrets. "That is what she called for."

"Then the Littlest Egret has the loudest voice!"
said Kudu. "I declare she is the winner!"

The next day, wherever Giraffe went he heard all
the animals on the Great Plain whispering,
"The Littlest Egret has the loudest voice!"

And he stayed very silent.

And so today Giraffe doesn't shout any more, and he certainly doesn't

HAW! HAW! HAW!

like he used to. He keeps quiet as quiet. But now and then Giraffe gives a little HRRRUMPH of a laugh and the other animals don't mind a bit.